7 SUCCESS SECRETS FOR PAPER CUP INDUSTRY

Essential Strategies You Need Today to Unleash Profitability & Growth.

7 SUCCESS SECRETS FOR PAPER CUP INDUSTRY

Essential Strategies You Need Today to Unleash Profitability & Growth.

Mohit M Agrawal

International Paper & Board Converting Strategist

Worldwide Published by
Pendown Press

PENDOWN PRESS LLP
An ISO 9001 & ISO 14001 Certified Co.
Regd. Office 3767A, Kanhaiya Nagar,
Tri Nagar, Delhi-110035
Ph.: 8180886000, 9650072927, 8595249536
E-mail: info@pendownpress.com
Branch Office 1A/2A, 20, Hari Sadan, Ansari Road,
Daryaganj, New Delhi-110002
Ph.: 011-45794768
Website: PendownPress.com

First Edition: 2023

ISBN: 978-93-5554-604-3

Layout and Cover Designed by Pendown Graphics Team
Printed and Bound in India by Thomson ress India Ltd.

I dedicate this book to my parents,
Mr. Madan Lal Agrawal
and Mrs. Prem Lata Agrawal,
whose love, care, and nurturing
have brought me to the level I stand
at today. Also the unwavering
support of my wife Nishita
& my kids - Hitanshi & Khush
and their belief in me are my greatest
sources of strength.

Contents

About Me i

Gratitude ii

Who is this for? iii

My Promise iv

My Journey v

Why did I write this Book? vi

Chapter 1
Start of Paper Converting Business 1

Chapter 2
How we did trials and it broke us 4

Chapter 3
When We called Experts 5

Chapter 4
How Industry work? 7

Chapter 5
Type of Paper Cups 8

Chapter 6
Problems in Paper Cups Industry 10

Chapter 7
Effect of these problems 11

Chapter 8
Solution ?												14

Chapter 9
What is Intelligent Buying Framework?					15

Chapter 10
Reduce Cost & Increase Product Acceptability			19

Bonus Chapter #1
Quality Control in Paper Cup Industry					37

Chapter 11
Case Study											39

Chapter 12
What is Upcoming-Sustainability						42

Chapter 13
The Big Thing About Paper Cup Machines?				47

Chapter 14
Testimonials											51

Closure												54
Mission												55
Challenge											56
My Another Must Read Book
For Brand Owners										57

About Me

I am an Indian entrepreneur and an international "Paper Converting Strategist" with an experience of more than 10 years in the industry.

I am also one of the Youngest Chartered Accountants of India & currently serving as the CEO of Jagannath Industries Pvt. Ltd. and Director of Jagannath Group of Companies.

I have created the "Intelligent Buying Framework" for helping the business owners & procurement heads of the paper based food service product industry like Cups, Plates, Box, Tubs etc.

Gratitude

Mr. Akshar Yadav (AY)

I am thankful to My Mentor Mr. Akshar Yadav, my Parents, my team, and Mr. Dinesh Verma, who motivated me to write this book.

Mr. Akshar Yadav helped me to establish my name in the Industry & making me Expert of Paper & Board Converting industry.

Who is this for?

- The upcoming Paper Cup Manufacturing companies who need education on this business.
- The Existing Paper Cup Producers across Globe Specially USA, Europe, Saudi & Middle East having high speed & medium speed machines.
- Those willing to grow their business & profits
- Those willing to expand their view point towards the business & Industry
- Those willing to learn more about what they do everyday (Paper Cup Manufacturing) and understand What is wrong, What is right and What is better to do.

This is for all the Business Owners, CEOs, Procurement Heads of Paper Cup & Food Service Product Industry.

My Promise

After reading this book any Paper Product Industry owner or procurement heads will not end up buying the wrong product.

You will never end up causing damage to your supply chain, brands, market & goodwill.

You will have only profits and growth in business because of the right product & service.

You will be able to-

1. Reduce your Inventory cost & Never Get Stock Out

2. Reduce your Wastage by upto 3%

3. Grow your profits & happiness index with 5M Framework

My Journey

When I was about to finish my exams in 2008, I received a call from my uncle asking me to come to his city and help him set up his new factory. It was a great opportunity for me to learn about the industry.

It turned out to be one of the best experiences of my life. Over the next 6 months, I worked with him to set up North India's largest Salt Refinery in 2009. We work day & night, and we were able to start operation with worked time of 6 months.

During Those 6 months, I learned how to interact with people, how to communicate effectively, how to make deals, and gained knowledge about machinery and their functioning. I also built relationships with hundreds of people.

When I started my own business

After completing my studies in Chartered Accountancy and graduating in 2011, I began immersing myself in the packaging material Industry. After learning for 2 years, I started my own business of BOPP Woven Bags in 2013.

Why did I write this Book?

So, we were engaged in the business of packaging materials and coated papers for the food service industry, and everything was going smoothly.

However, one day, I started to feel that something was amiss. There was no joy in the repetitive routine of doing the same things in the same way every day.

I was in a dilemma about how to improve my life and make it happier. Feeling uncertain, I turned to my mentor for guidance.

My mentor advised me to go and meet my clients and other industry players. He said, keep - emphasised that everyone in the industry was facing unsolved problems, and they couldn't see beyond those challenges.

He told me to identify their problems and provide them with solutions.

And here the story starts...

Chapter 1

Start of Paper Converting Business

In our company, we were engaged in the production of PP Woven Bags for the Packaging Industry. We had one extrusion coating line in that unit.

Once I had the opportunity to visit a company located in Vapi, a city in the western part of India. This particular company was doing production of Soap Wrappers and PE Coated Soap Stiffeners.

The visit to this company was quite good and interesting. During my visit, I found a similar machine we also had in our factory.

A well set up company with excellent infrastructure it was and very inspiring as they grew their business by multifold in the last 3 years.

In the evening, we drove back to Ahmedabad (Gujarat) and reached our hotel late at night.

After a few weeks, an individual from my city contacted me and asked for a meeting to discuss matters related to paper business.

At that time, I was uncertain about the purpose of the meeting, but I agreed to visit his place and meet him.

"Okay, you are welcome". He said.

Next morning, I went to his modest office located near the city center of Jaipur, famously known as the pink city of India.

It was a small office belonging to his friend, a Paper scrap dealer who was dealing in newspaper scraps.

After a Chai (Tea) he started.

"Mr. Mohit, do you have an Extrusion Coating Machine Line" he asked?

"Yes", I replied.

"Great. Can you take up a job for us?" he asked.

"What kind of job?" I asked.

"We have Paper Cup Manufacturing machines, and for that we need paper," he explained.

"Okay". I nodded in agreement.

"This Paper is Cupstock Board, and it has Extrusion Coated Polyethylene on it. This is a very technical job that requires a large machine, and you happen to have that machine," he said.

"You can purchase paper from this company," he said, providing me with their contact information. "Produce some sample quantities for us, and if they are approved, we can establish a good business."

"Okay. I will try it for you," I replied. I took the basic details and came back to my home.

Chapter 2

How we did trials and it broke us

I arranged to buy a sample quantity of paper from a local paper dealer in our city.

Upon reaching the factory, I rolled up my sleeves and started a production trial with my team.

We attempted to run the paper on the machine for an hour but we failed.

I didn't give up there. I encouraged my team by saying, "Let's try again!"

Throughout the entire day, we persisted in our efforts, but by the end of the day, we still couldn't succeed.

The Paper was getting torn before rewinding.

We were now frustrated.

Chapter 3

When We called Experts

It took me another three weeks to get new paper rolls, as the previous lot was completely wasted.

This time I requested and arranged for the visit of three expert individuals from different parts of Gujarat.

The first expert was a machinery control specialist, one of the top professionals in India.

The second expert was the person who built my machine.

The third expert was an experienced machine technician who had expertise in operating the same type of product.

We started the day at 8:30 am, and did all the adjustments and trials. The material was being wasted, which left me feeling increasingly frustrated.

In the night, around 22:15, when I was just doing all the hits & trials with my idea, suddenly I made a small change in the rewinding process, and like magic, everything fell into place. Everyone was overjoyed to witness the successful production of a flawless roll. The machine was now running smoothly, and a sense of relief washed over us all.

The paper roll was getting bigger and it was our last remaining roll of paper, as all other material had already been wasted.

Finally we all were relaxed and happy that their visit and the full day of hard work finally gave the desired results.

The following day, I presented the samples to the original buyer, who examined them and approved the quality.

&

I was overjoyed, feeling like I was on the 7th sky....

From that day until now, we have continued to produce that product with even greater expertise & dedication.

Throughout the years, we have made a lot of mistakes and learned invaluable lessons from each one.

Chapter 4

How Industry work?

Paper Cup Industry Flow Chart

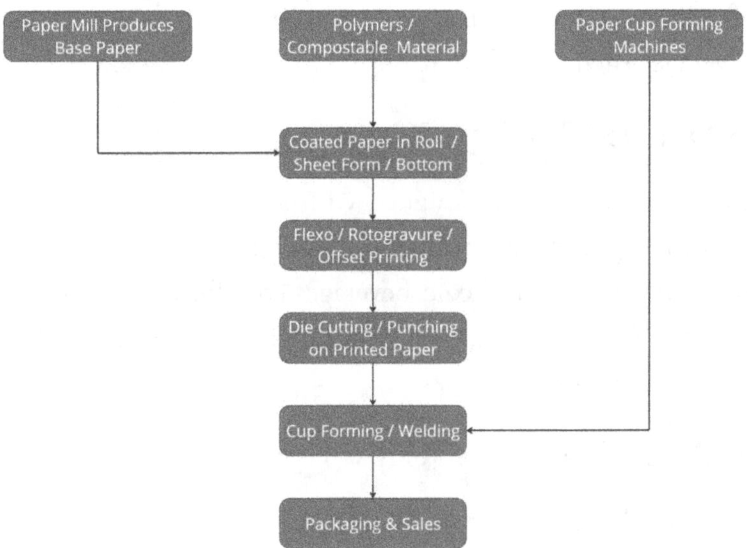

Chapter 5

Type of Paper Cups

1. Single-Wall Paper Cups

These are the most basic type and are made from a single layer of paper. They are suitable for serving both hot and cold beverages such as coffee, tea, soft drinks, and water.

2. Double-Wall Paper Cups

Double-wall cups are designed with an additional insulating layer to improve heat insulation. This extra layer helps to keep hot beverages hot and cold beverages cold for a longer period of time. They offer better insulation and reduce the need for additional cup sleeves.

3. Ripple-Wall Paper Cups

Ripple-wall cups have a unique textured outer layer that provides enhanced insulation and a comfortable grip. The ripple design acts as an additional insulating layer, making them suitable for serving hot drinks without the need for cup sleeves.

4. Cold Cups

Cold cups are specifically designed for serving chilled beverages such as iced coffee, smoothies, soft drinks, and iced tea. They are typically made from thicker paper or have a 2-side polyethylene coating to prevent condensation and leakage.

5. Ice Cream Cups

These cups are specifically designed for serving ice cream, frozen yogurt, and other frozen desserts. They are often made from sturdy paper or have a 2-side polyethylene coating to withstand the low temperatures and prevent leakage.

6. Disposable Food Containers

Although not strictly cups, disposable food containers made from paper are also widely used. They come in various shapes and sizes, they are ideal for serving a range of food items soups, salads, snacks, and take-out meals.

Chapter 6

Problems in Paper Cups Industry

95% of Paper Cup Producers I have met in the last 7 years across 10 countries have been facing similar challenges and obstacles in their business.

I met a lot of companies in India, USA, Middle East, Africa, Europe, I observed that everyone was struggling to grow their business.

The common problems were like below -

- Very Low or No Profits
- No Happiness in doing this business
- Excessive mental pressure
- Financial crunch
- Cut throat competition
- Unstable employee retention.
- Difficulty in finding skilled and experienced team members
- Not able to increase sales with profits
- Rejection in quality of paper cups from customer after delivery
- & so on…

Chapter 7

Effect of these problems

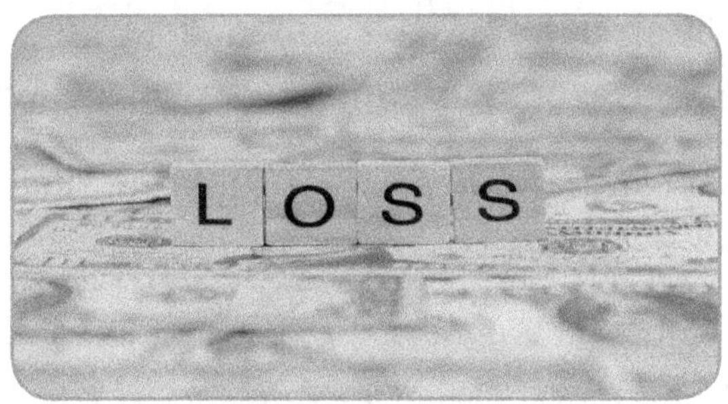

- Loss of Money
- Loss of Time
- Loss of Happiness
- Loss of Enthusiasm
- Loss of Customers

Loss of Money

Business owners suffer financial losses due to these problems in their businesses.

Many small business owners exhaust their working capital within a few months or years of operating under such circumstances, leading to a financial crunch.

This financial crunch significantly impacts both their business and personal lives.

According to several business owners, this problem is currently impeding their families and destroying their dreams.

Loss of Time

These problems leads to the loss of time, which is the most crucial element in our lives.

The constant engagement in fire-fighting and the ineffective handling of these issues consume valuable time.

As a result, you are unable to focus on customer service, growth plans, and execution strategies.

Loss of Happiness

It all begins with finding happiness in your work, which will take you to new heights.

If you are content in your business, it will reflect in your family as well. You will have the strength and excitement to serve your customers wholeheartedly, going above and beyond.

If you are unhappy in your business, you inadvertently create unseen barriers for yourself, your team, and most importantly, your customers.

Loss of Enthusiasm

Zeal & Enthusiasm are the key drivers in both life & business, capable of propelling you to new heights.

Unfortunately, this is one of the biggest element missing in the industry and among business owners.

Due to low profits and poor growth, they are losing the joy associated with their business.

The impact of this loss of enthusiasm can be clearly observed among the teams and workers within these businesses. Ultimately, it diminishes productivity and negatively affects customer service once again.

Loss of Customers

This is a situation that nobody desires, yet is a bitter truth.

If you reflect on your past or even the present state of your business, you may notice that you have lost valuable and significant customers due to poor quality or sub par customer service, which is deeply disheartening.

Acquiring these customers requires significant effort, and it is disheartening when they eventually depart due to our own minor mistakes.

I have also faced the same in the past and it hurts the most.

Chapter 8

Solution ?

"Intelligent Buying Framework"

After visiting numerous customers & industry players and understanding their problems in detail, I started working on the solution.

I did a lot of research, studied various research papers, and discussed with the industry experts & engineers.

I also underwent a 10-month long training on "Managing a Manufacturing Business with correct processes, procedures, & systems."

I underwent very deep training under my mentor to resolve the problems related to marketing & sales. This training opened up new avenues to solve these problems which were unresolved till date for so many companies across the world.

Chapter 9

What is Intelligent Buying Framework?

Intelligent Buying Framework (IBF™) serve as the ultimate solution for the business owners, CEOs and procurement managers in the industry. It emphasizes the importance of implementing the right process and techniques to procure the correct materials at the appropriate frequency and with the right quality parameters.

IBF™ is assisting industry owners and procurement heads in making responsible purchases with ease, at reduced cost, and time deliveries.

IBF™ is becoming so popular among this fraternity due to its ease of doing, simplicity & implementable action points.

IBF™ holds valuable secrets that are critical for numerous business owners and procurement heads. Understanding and acting upon these secrets immediately can lead to transformative changes in their current situations, propelling them towards growth.

Secret #1: Clear Old Stocks

Always work on FIFO Basis.

FIFO (First in, first out): It means always use and finish the material that was first bought & received in stock.

It is advisable to avoid using new materials first. This practice would result in keeping the older materials in stock, eventually leading to a decline in their quality. Factors such as moisture loss, increased stiffness, and decreased-ply bond strength of the paper board can negatively impact the older materials.

> *"This habit of FIFO will save you from dead stock and minimize the risk of material getting damaged due to non-usage since a very long time."*

What is present practice? - The current practice is that the store person for his ease issues new material immediately upon demand by factory & again new inward happens and it piles up on the old stock. This prevents us from utilizing the old stock, which eventually deteriorates and becomes damaged.

For working under FIFO basis, you need to correct the storage process of raw materials. If you have sufficient storage space, it is recommended to stock the new lot in a separate area, ensuring it is stored over & above the older rolls or sheet pallets.

However, if you are limited on storage space, there are steps you can take:

1. Firstly, ensure your purchases align with '**Our Stock Management Tool**', which helps maintain optimum and minimum inventory levels in your warehouse, avoiding the issue of over stacking.

2. Store the materials in a manner that facilitates the easy issuance of the older stock by store personnel. Many companies have started implemented palletised storage systems to enhance the movement of goods and improve accessibility.

Another benefit of this process is that you can always calculate the actual cost of production of each lot based on the materials used in that specific order.

Once you begin calculating the costs, you can start generating profits.

Secret #2: Fix Purchase Price with CIF Terms

This is the latest practice which is saving huge money to the companies in our Industry.

> *"The only person who can get the best shipping cost offer from the shipping line is the SHIPPER & not the consignee."*

Often, buyers attempt to be clever by fixing the FOB terms, assuming that they will get the shipping cost less than the shipper and they arrange bookings through their own agency.

Always they end up paying higher shipping costs and get involved in extensive documentation processes, which hampers their pocket & consumes their time.

Always give the task of container booking to the shipper because the shipping point agency possesses better negotiation power to obtain the most favorable sea cost.

"A dollar saved is a dollar earned"

Try it and you will see results.

Chapter 10

Reduce Cost & Increase Product Acceptability

Secret #3: Game of High Bulk & Low Bulk Paper

What is high bulk and low bulk?

First, we need to understand what Bulk/Caliper?

Bulk/Caliper is a unit to measure the thickness of Paper.

But thickness is not GSM. GSM is its volumetric unit.

Formula =

GSM x Bulk Ratio = Micron of Paper

Example -

A.   300 GSM Paper x 1.25 Bulk = 375 Microns

B.   250 GSM Paper x 1.50 Bulk = 375 Microns

In "A" - GSM is higher but wonderful thing is that "B" is always a better paper in terms of strength and stiffness.

There is an old belief that places utmost importance on the weight of each cup for buyers. Buyers tend to compare cups solely-based on their respective weights assuming that a heavier cup equates to a superior product.

It says that if your cup weight is higher, then it is a complete & good cup.

However, this belief is misguided.

We are changing and changing this belief by educating business owners about the concept of "High Bulk - Low Bulk."

Through this education, they are making efforts to inform their customers about the quality and strength of the cup, even when it has a lighter weight.

Always what matters is the Strength of the Cup and It comes from the Thickness of the Paper (Not GSM)

Customers love the cups made of High Bulk Paper & You can save money by using lesser GSM of Paper along with getting the same or better strength in that cup.

See this image showing curling thickness of both type of cups with the same GSM of paper.

Thicker Curling will give higher cup strength and is more suitable for using Lids on the top of cups.

High Bulk (Thick urling)   **Low Bulk (Thin urling)**

*"We have been in Industry for the last
5 decades & We never knew these things
about the Paper (Our Raw Material).*

*Its First time someone (Mohit M Agrawal) has
guided us in such detail about our Industry and
our material and he knows it better than us."*

-Demos Papadimas,

National Director, Superior Cups, USA

Why Right Bulk of Paper is Important.

Paper bulk is an important factor for paper cups as it directly affects the strength, insulation properties, and overall quality of the cup. Here's why paper bulk is significant:

1. **Strength and Durability:**

   To withstand handling and usage requirements, paper cups need to be strong and durable.

   A higher paper bulk indicates a thicker and denser paper, which provides better structural integrity to the cup.

   Cups made from paper with higher bulk are less likely to tear, puncture, or easily deform, ensuring that they can hold liquids without leakage or collapsing.

2. **Insulation:**

   Maintaining the temperature of the beverages is crucial for paper cups. The bulkier the paper, the better its insulating properties.

   Higher paper bulk helps to create an additional air gap between the layers, acting as a thermal barrier and reducing heat transfer.

   This helps in keeping hot beverages hot and cold beverages cold for a longer duration.

3. **Printability:**

    The bulk of the paper can affect the print quality and ink absorption. With higher paper bulk, there is better ink coverage, sharper printing, and vibrant colors.

    This is particularly important for cups with custom branding or printed designs, enhancing their visual appeal and marketing potential.

4. **Stiffness and Shape Retention:**

    Paper cups should maintain their shape and rigidity during use. Higher paper bulk contributes to the stiffness of the cup, allowing it to hold its shape even when filled with liquid. This helps prevent cup deformation, maintains a professional appearance, and ensure ease of use for consumers.

5. **Customer Perception:**

    The thickness and overall quality of the paper cup impact customer perception. Cups made from paper with higher bulk are often associated with better quality and a premium feel. This positive perception can influence brand image and customer satisfaction.

    It is important to note that the required paper bulk for paper cups may vary depending on the specific cup size, design, and intended usage.

Secret #4 : Importance of Roll Core ID

What is Roll ID and Roll OD?

See the picture below to understand the dimensions.

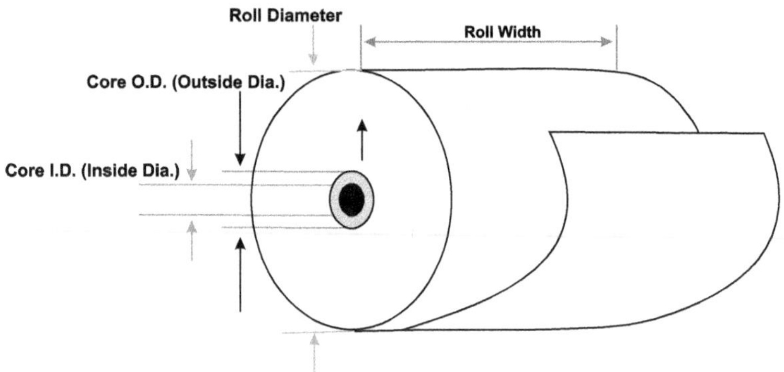

Always ask your supplier to use at least 6" (152 mm) paper core i.e. Roll ID should be at least 152 mm.

But why?

Because it saves the roll' last paper wastage by at least 50%.

When you buy rolls on 3" core the last material layers around 5-6 kg in each roll gets so much curled due to high tension of the Paper roll of 500-700 kgs.

This material is never usable on printing or die punching machines due to its high curling.

Using a minimum 6" paper core in rolls can result in approximately 1% less wastage, directly increasing your profit by 1%.

Additionally, the chances of core damage are significantly higher with a 3" core diameter, especially if a roll falls or is mishandled.

Paper cores with a minimum thickness of 15 mm and a minimum diameter of 6" have the least chances of damage in case of any accident.

Surprisingly, many paper cup industries, including industry leaders, have not adopted this practice for years simply because their printing or punching machines were not supplied by with 6" or 8" air shafts initially.

However, those who have made the switch are saving a significant amount of money by reducing wastage. The savings resulting from this practice change are substantial.

Secret #5: Palletised Loading

This secret also seems like Not a Secret. This is a very generic concept.

Many companies are tempted to save money by opting for non-palletised loading or by using low cost & poor pallets. However, this practice result in financial losses and significant damage to material.

It is essential to always ask your supplier to provide material with strong-quality pallets. It is the supplier's responsibility to ensure this. Ask him about the loading capacity and strength of the pallets, as these same pallets can be utilized for material storage and handling in your warehouse.

Furthermore, it is advisable to ask the supplier to maintain a similar outer diameter for all rolls. This makes it easier to store them, even in small storage areas, by stacking one roll on top of another.

"We have saved good money by reducing at least 1% wastage of paper by lesser damage of paper during unloading, storage and movement in our factory with Mohit M Agrawal, compared to old suppliers who never used Pallets."

~Mr. Rafiq Sadi, Algeria

Secret #6 : Consistent Raw Material Brand

Your machine operators are habitual to run a specific type of paper on the cup making machines.

All the machines are set for this particular paper which is sourced FIRST in terms of speed, pressure, dwell time & temperature.

Everything is running smoothly.

Suddenly the operators are having a huge pile of wastage, there is reduced production and huge breakdown of machines & loss of productivity.

Why?

Strongest reason is that the Supplier of material has changed the brand and quality of the base paper which has been used.

This new paper has different bulk, roughness, bend strength, stiffness etc. for which your machine has not been set up.

Every time the Paper Brand Changes, you are going to lose a lot. Stick to one brand of paper which runs well and has zero machine downtime due to error of the supplier.

You should inquire with the supplier about the specific brand of paper, and it should remain consistent with each supply. Additionally, request the specification sheet of the base paper, including its brand. This practice will eliminate the chances of receiving the wrong or different brand of paper in your supplies.

Moreover, it is crucial to have quality testing facilities in your factory to ensure that the supplied paper is correct and matches the specification outlined in the specification sheet.

In the upcoming chapter, I will focus on the types of quality testing and their procedures, which are essential for any paper cup manufacturing unit to have.

Secret #7 : The 5M framework For Paper Cup Industry

1. Man

- Retain your high-performing team members. Regularly measure their performance and ensure that you do not let them go. They have been critical for your success thus far.

- Provide training to both your existing members and newcomers with the assistance of machine suppliers, material suppliers, and trained engineers. This will ensure that your organization always has a sufficient number of qualified individuals and reduce dependency on a few key individuals.

- Ensure that you have the right person for the right job. If someone is not performing well, assess whether they are suitable for the task at hand.

- Establish top-notch safety measures for your team. Ensure that the workforce has access to safety gears such as safety shoes, gloves, high-end earplugs to protect them from machine noise.

- Clearly define the hiring procedure and hire efficient workers who align with your company's vision. Before bringing anyone on board, share your company's vision with them and ensure they are aligned with it. Once they understand and embrace the vision, they will be more likely to excel on their roles for the benefit of the company.

2. Machine

- Create preventive maintenance checklists for all machines and implement a preventive maintenance schedule. Preventive maintenance can significantly reduce machine breakdowns, saving up to 64% in the industry.

- Ensure that machines are kept free from wear and tear. Do not ignore any issue that arise with the machine, As even small problems can escalate and disrupt production.

- Regularly inspect and maintain all gears, heaters, molds, switches, temperature meters, and thermocouples according to preventive maintenance schedule. Always keep spare machine parts in stock for each machine.

- If you do not already have them, obtain the list of spare parts and preventive maintenance checklist from the machine supplier. These resources are essential for effective maintenance and can help ensure smooth operations.

- Hire a Problem Solver for your factory who is capable of handling various issues, similar to how a business owner would. This individual will help you stay away from day-today problems, allowing you to focus on marketing, which is your primary responsibility.

3. Material

- Create and adhere to a quality control (QC) checklist for raw materials implement stringent quality checks on incoming paper and only release it for production after it has passed QC standards. These checks should focus on heat sealability, GSM testing, and micron testing. This will require the use of appropriate testing equipment.

- Establish and follow a QC checklist for cups in production, conducting random testing on an hourly basis for each machine. This involves checking curling, sealing, and conducting leakage tests.

- Prepare & follow a QC checklist for finished products – Before packing and dispatching, conduct random testing on the ready cups, focusing on printing, forming, sealing, leakage test. And ensuring the correct counting of cups in sleeves. This is crucial for maintaining your brand value.

- To carry out these testing processes, hire a dedicated QC team and Implement the a fore mentioned checklists. Small-scale industries often runs away from hiring QC teams due to perceived additional costs, but investing in a QC team can save you from potential significant losses.

- Install an Auto Defect Detection System on machines prior to collection and packing. This system utilizes cameras to conduct visual inspection from multiple angles and automatically removes any defective cups, directing them to a separate collection point.

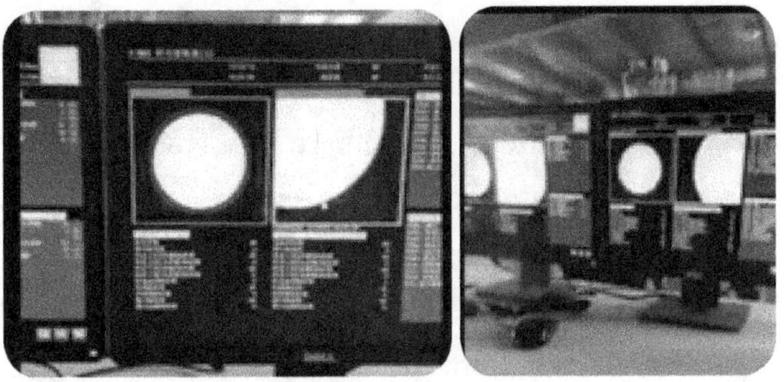

4. Money

- It is highly recommended for small or medium-scale industries to establish a reserve account and transfer minimum of 20% of monthly profits into this account on a consistent basis. While starting this habit may not be difficult, maintaing it can be challenging. However, those who follow this practice are able to accumulate significant reserves over time. These reserves serve as a safeguard during times of crisis and provide the necessary funds for new investment without facing financial constraints.

- It is advisable to limit the credit period given to customers. Implement a CRM system and hire a dedicated person to ensure timely follow-up and collection of payments from customers on time every time. This single action will DELETE your cash crunch from the business. In fact, we have witnessed a 400% increase in collections when a CRM is utilized for follow-up and reminders to customers.

- Stay updated with the industry to reduce the cost of purchase. Keep in touch with suppliers and stay informed about paper and raw material prices. Subscribe a couple of paper industry newsletters for price trend updates. This will enable you to make informed purchasing decisions and potentially lower your procurement costs

5. Market

- Choose your customers wisely. Select customers who not only provide higher sales but also bring in higher profits and show respect and appreciation for your business.

Customer Classification

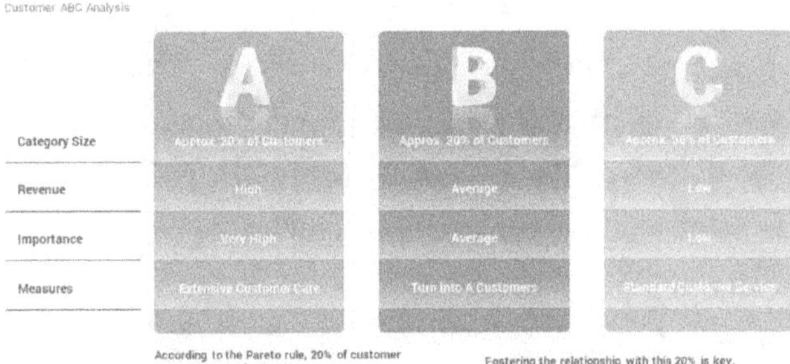

- In general, there are 3 types of customers:

    A. These customers bring higher sales, higher profits, show respect and love towards your business, provide references, and make timely payment.

    B. This category represents customers who fall within average parameters across various factors.

    C. Everything is poor here in this case.

        Ideally, you should strive to have only customers in category A.

Category B is not a distinct category, so customers falling under this classification should either be transitioned to category A by adhering to the rules and expectations or moved to category C.

It is crucial to note that working with category C customers is highly discouraged.

Therefore, it is advisable to cease working with category C customers altogether, as they are unlikely to contribute positively to your business's growth and financial success.

— If you import materials, it is advisable to export a minimum of 50% of your production. This practice serves as a natural hedge, safeguarding your business from any currency fluctuations.

— Even if you don't import, it is still recommended to aim for 30-40% of your products being exported. This strategy allows you to maintain control over your sales and aligns with the principle, **"Don't Put All Your Eggs in One Basket"**. Diversifying your customer base and markets will aid in better cash management and mitigate risks.

Quality Control in Paper Cup Industry

In this chapter, I will discuss the quality test, the necessary instruments required for conducting these tests, and the testing process that is crucial for the paper cup industry.

Raw material tests:

- GSM Test of Coated Board
- GSM Test of PE Film
- GSM Test of Uncoated Board
- Thickness Test of Paper
- Bulk Test of Paper
- Heat Sealing test

Required Instruments:

- GSM Cutter & Rubber Pad
- Weigh Scale - Calibrated
- Chemical - Ethyl Cello solve
- Safety Gloves - Thin & Lab Grade
- Micrometer
- Calculator

- Heat Seal Testing Machine

WIP & Finished material tests:

- Heat Sealing of Cups

- Leakage Test

- Ink Rub Test for Printing

- Cup Strength Test

Required Instruments:

- Table with Glass Bottom and Cup Shape Cut Outs

- Hot Water & coffee kettle

- Compression Strength Tester for Checking Cup Strength

I will be writing another instabook soon, specifically focusing on quality testing procedures. This instabook will provide comprehensive guidance and will be accompanied by a specially crafted testing instrument, which will be made available to those who require it.

Chapter 11

Case Study

Why Quality Control is Important to Learn?

During my USA visit in March 2023, I had the opportunity to meet with several Paper Cup Producers. These companies had been using Poly Coated Paper from US Paper Mills for many decades and never tried the imported Paper from India.

During the visit, I obtained a few samples of US-based Paper Mills from these Cup Producers and I asked them to get these tested at an approved laboratory.

However, they were unsure about which laboratory to use and which tests to conduct for the samples. Taking the initiative, I brought these samples with me and brought them to India and conducted all the necessary tests in our own laboratory.

The results were very much surprising. I was also shocked to see these kinds of Quality Results.

Here we can see the results of QC tests of US Based Paper Mills, along with a comparison to Indian paper for manufacturing paper cups.

Material Quality Comparison Sheet on parameters of Thickness & GSM of Paper							
Samples - EG Packaging USA							
Samples - Jagannath Industries Pvt Ltd, Gandhidham, Gujarat, India							
	A	**B**	**C**	**D**	**E**	**F**	**G**	**H**
Item	Caliper EG - Claimed	Caliper EG - Actual	GSM EG - Claimed	GSM EG - Actual	Difference - Loss of Material	Micron EG - Claimed	Micron EG - Actual	Difference - Less Microns %
Side Wall Roll	14.00	12.80	268	290	8.21%	356	325	8.68%
Side Wall Roll	15.00	14.06	278	300	7.91%	381	357	6.37%
Side Wall Roll	18.00	16.14	318	340	6.92%	458	410	10.39%
Average				Loss-->	7.68%			8.48%

	I	**J**	**K**	**L**	**M**	**N**	**O**	**P**
Item	Caliper JIPL - Claimed	Caliper JIPL - Actual	GSM JIPL - Claimed	GSM JIPL - Actual	Difference - Loss of Material	Micron JIPL - Claimed	Micron JIPL - Actual	Difference - Less Microns %
Side Wall Roll	14.00	13.81	268	262	-2.24%	356	351	1.40%
Side Wall Roll	15.00	15.26	288	285	-1.04%	381	388	-1.84%
Side Wall Roll	17.00	16.84	330	326	-1.21%	432	428	0.93%
Average				Savings-->	-1.50%			0.16%

Savings on Material With JIPL Paper	(E - M)	9.18%	(H - P)	8.32%

If a company buys every month Paper at an average of	300	Tons
Ultimate Loss they are making now with EG Paper @ 9.18%	23.04	Tons
If US Material Price of this Paper upto your factory is	$1,800.00	Per Ton
Monthly Loss with EG Packaging Paper in this case	$41,473.55	
Annual Loss with EG Packaging Paper in this case	$497,682.65	

Note - Samples taken from a Cup Producer in Ohio who was using material of EG Packaging since more than 10 years.

After this incident, we have established a Paper Cup & Paper Samples Testing Service available to anyone in the industry from any part of the world. The best part is that this service is completely free of cost.

If you wish to have your paper samples tested and receive detailed test results, simply send us your samples, and we will conduct the necessary testings for you. Once completed, we will provide you with a comprehensive report detailing the materials and their properties.

To avail of this service, please fill out the form located at-

bit.ly/FreePaperTestingByJIPL

or scan this QR Code.

Alternatively, you can send us an email at-

paper@jagannathindustries.com

Chapter 12

What is Upcoming-Sustainability

The next big thing is Compostable Paper Cups & Recyclable Paper Cups & Food service Products.

Types of compostable paper cups:

Compostable paper cups are specifically designed to break down into compost or organic matter under certain conditions. Here are some common types of compostable paper cups:

Here are 3 main categories of compostable & recyclable paper cups:

1. **PLA-lined Paper Cups:** PLA stands for poly lactic acid, which is a biodegradable and compostable material derived from renewable resources like cornstarch or sugarcane. PLA-lined paper cups have an inner lining made of PLA, providing a barrier against liquid absorption. These cups are compostable under commercial composting conditions.

2. **PE-lined Paper Cups:** PE refers to polyethylene, which is a type of plastic. However, some paper cups are lined with a thin layer of PE that helps prevent liquid leakage. While the paper portion of the cup may be compostable,

the PE lining needs to be separated and disposed of separately in recycling facilities that accept plastic film.

3. **BioPBS-lined Paper Cups:** BioPBS is a biodegradable and compostable polymer derived from renewable resources. BioPBS-lined paper cups are compostable under specific composting conditions and can break down into organic matter.

It's important to note that the compostability of these cups relies on specific composting conditions, including factors such as temperature, humidity, and microbial activity.

Compostable paper cups should be disposed of in composting facilities that can provide the necessary conditions for proper decomposition.

When selecting compostable paper cups, it is advisable to look for certifications or labels such as the "Compostable" logo or certifications like the ASTM D6400 or EN 13432 standards. These certifications indicate that the cups meet specific compostability criteria and can be composted in appropriate facilities.

It is must to follow local waste management guidelines and composting regulations to ensure proper disposal and composting of compostable paper cups in your region.

Recyclable Material

Any paper cup or its waste or paper production waste which can be collected and recycled into paper again is called recyclable material.

These material are typically either PE Coated or PP coated for heat sealability.

Here is some information about these cups:

1. **Polyethylene (PE) Coated Paper Cups:** Paper cups have a thin coating of polyethylene on the inner surface, which provides a moisture barrier. These cups can be recycled in facilities that accept polyethylene-coated paper products. The PE coating needs to be separated during the recycling process.

2. **Polypropylene (PP) Coated Paper Cups:** Some paper cups have a polypropylene coating on the inner surface, which provides liquid resistance.

3. These cups can be recycled in facilities that accept polypropylene-coated paper products. Similar to PE-coated cups, the PP coating needs to be separated during recycling.

However, separating the PP or PE film is not always practical and feasible for companies on a large scale. As a result, there was a need for a solution that eliminates the need for PE/PP film coatings inside the cup.

Then the Aqueous coating was developed.

These cup materials are made of Aqueous emulsion coating material, which is applied using new machines that cannot be used with conventional machines.

While this material may or may not be compostable, it can be easily recycled by putting it into the re-pulper section of any paper mill The aqueous coating can be readily washed out into the re-pulper.

This material is both heat sealable and ultrasonic sealable, depending on machine speed and paper GSM.

Understand the basic differences between all categories.

Basis	Compostable	Biodegradable	Recyclable
Availability	Easy	Not Available	Easy
Certification	4-8 Months	>18 months	4 Months
End Disposal	Home/Industrial Compostable	Natural Bio Degradation	Recycling for Paper Pulp
Process of Disposal	In Our Control	Beyond Control, Not Practical	Repulping by Paper Mills
Type of Material	PLA, PBS, Bagasse Based	Bioplastics Based	Aqueous Coatings

Product Mix Example to make it Compostable:

Paper Cup Producers often encounter a challenge when they have compostable cups available, but the customer demanda complete package with compostable features.

You can produce a PLA Coated Paper Cup/Bowl/Tub.

If you need to add a Lid for that, you can use Bagasse-Based Lid in combination. Bagasse-based products are completely compostable and made from agricultural products.

It will give you a complete compostable product package & yes that is REAL SUSTAINABLE.

Like this, you can also consider using paper straws, which are made without any PE coatings and are both recyclable and compostable.

Chapter 13

The Big Thing
About Paper Cup Machines?

Super High Speed Machines...

Many Industry Players are using machines with speed of 60-120 Pcs Per Minute.

But the industry has advanced to machines capable of producing up to 330 Pcs/Minute.

Leaders Like - Horauf & PMC are producing these super high-speed Machines to produce top quality with **Least Cost of Production to cope up the market demand with Limited Human Resources.**

Low Speed machines are from China, India & Korea.

High Speed machines are mainly from Germany & USA.

Super high-speed paper cup machines are advanced manufacturing machines specifically designed to produce paper cups at an extremely fast rate. These machines offer numerous advantages that make them popular in the paper cup industry.

Here are some key benefits of super high-speed paper cup machines:

1. **Increased production speed:** These machines excel in their ability to operate at significantly higher speeds compared to conventional paper cup machines. They can produce a large number of cups per minute, significantly improving overall production efficiency and meeting high-demand requirements.

2. **Improved productivity:** With faster production speeds, super high-speed paper cup machines empower manufacturers to achieve higher productivity levels of productivity. This can lead to increased output, shorter lead times, and the capability to fulfill large orders within tight deadlines.

3. **Cost-effective:** The higher production speed and improved productivity of these machines directly contribute to cost savings. By producing more cups in less time, manufacturers can optimize their resources, reduce labor costs, and enhance overall operational efficiency.

4. **Enhanced automation:** Super high-speed paper cup machines often come equipped with cutting-edge-automation features, such as automatic cup feeding, bottom punching, and sealing mechanisms. These

automated processes minimize manual intervention, reduce the human error, and ensure consistent cup quality throughout the production process.

5. **Quality control:** These machines are designed to maintain high- quality standards even when operating at high speeds. They incorporate precise control systems to ensure accurate cup dimensions, proper sealing, and reliable cup forming. This helps to deliver consistent and reliable cup quality to end-users.

6. **Versatility:** Many super high-speed paper cup machines offer the flexibility to produce a variety of cup sizes and designs. These machines can efficiently handle different paper thicknesses, coatings, and printing requirements. As a result, manufacturers can meet the diverse needs and market demands of their customers.

7. **Energy efficiency:** With advancements in technology, modern high-speed paper cup machines are designed to be energy-efficient. They incorporate energy-saving features and optimized power consumption to reduce operating costs and environmental impact.

When considering the purchase of a super high-speed paper cup machine, it's essential to evaluate factors such as machine reliability, maintenance requirements, after-sales service, and available technical support. Taking these factors into account ensures a smooth and efficient operation of the machine.

Additionally, conducting a comprehensive cost-benefit analysis specific to your production needs will help assess the suitability and potential return on investment for such machines.

Remember to consult with industry experts, machine manufacturers, and existing users to gather comprehensive insights and make an informed decision for your business requirements.

Chapter 14

Testimonials

~Gerald Grimes,

President, IDM Products, Dallas, Tx, USA

"Mohit is our preferred & reliable supplier from India & we love doing business with him.

He serves us the Top Quality & Service with on time delivery.

He has become our most trusted partner now & he always focus on cost reduction & quality upgradation.

Our company just loves working with him as he always puts efforts on our growth."

***

~Animesh Humar,

Founder & CEO, Paricott India Paper Cups Pvt Ltd, India

"Mr. Mohit Agrawal, CEO of Jagannath Industries Pvt Ltd has always been our most preferred supplier.

As a prominent manufacturer of paper cups, it is imperative for Paricott to rely on top-notch suppliers, and he has consistently exceeded our expectations with commitment to excellence and unwavering dedication to quality.

His Expert Knowledge Base & his team's Exceptional Customer Service as being prompt in responding to our inquiries, providing accurate information and addressing any challenges has helped us to grow multifold in the last few years."

***

~Zhan Amiraghyan,

Production Head, Oval Paper Cups, Armenia

"Mohit has been my supplier and a great friend. Apart from being a supplier he is very supportive in many areas for my company."

"They have clarity on quality and terms, Their CRM gives top quality service and real time information about each step of our order from PO to delivery."

"I found them with Both White and Kraft Paper and they have been very supportive in providing samples before each quality approval. This makes us tension free about our imports."

Closure

Although I have tried to write and focus on all the most significant problems and provide their ideal solutions to save from losses and foster business growth through the proper selection of Paper Material and intelligent buying.

However, due to space limitations and other constraints, I could only include the key aspects in this writing.

If you really want to solve your problems and are looking for the expert help to remove your obstacles, fix any day for a coffee meet and let's talk in detail and plan to grow your business with me.

Mohit M Agrawal

Cell +91 98871 22262

md@jagannathindustries.com

Mission

I am on a mission to revolutionize the industry by empowering business owners and procurement heads by educating them and making them strong enough that they never require my assistance again.

I have a dream to foster the growth of the industry by enhancing productivity, improving product appeal, and supporting the advancement of all players within the industry.

I have a dream to grow the industry by increased productivity, product appeal and growth of the players in the industry.

Most importantly, the main goal of this journey is to minimize wastage of raw materials, resources, efforts, and time.

Challenge

Let's take the challenge.

Don't just read and put this book aside.

I hope I was able to create awareness and ignite the fire inside you to protect and grow your business and improve your product's standards.

Take the challenge and be the change you want.

Be the change and become the face of your industry.

Let's work on transforming the business with the framework I have presented.

Get learning of these critical things and show the result by implementing.

You know what?

I am always there to provide assistance and support to those who take action.

Good Luck. 05:15 am - 16/05/2023, Jaipur, India

My Another Must Read Book For Brand Owners

"This is a complete guide for Right selection of your Packaging material & how you can save money with that. It's a masterpiece."

~Naveen N Banura,

Chairman, M N Fashions

NOTES:

NOTES: